SAILING

Written By:
Herbert I. Kavet

Illustrated By:
Martin Riskin

Ivory Tower Publishing Co., Inc.
125 Walnut Street
P.O. Box 9132
Watertown, MA 02272-9132
Telephone #: (617) 923-1111   Fax #: (617) 923-8839

"Of course Herbert can handle a boat. He's been sailing since he was a little boy."

"We can't abandon ship. There are still four beers left."

Heads

Heads, as everyone knows, are seagoing toilets — only toilets are different because in toilets you just flush — while in heads, you need a mechanical engineering degree to make the bad stuff go away. Assuming first of all you can squeeze your behind into the head, which for some reason on a boat is about the size of a Kleenex box, you then have to throw levers and turn valves and pumps. You do this all in an exact sequence or the thing that looks like a toilet turns into a shower or microwave or ice maker, or overflows.

Heads

When anyone but the captain uses a head, it will become blocked. The captain must then delve into the thing to unblock it unless he can convince a crew member to do it. The crew members, if they have any brains, will all feign total ignorance since this is a very messy job.

Captains are captains by dint of their being smart enough to hold their usage of the head until they are safely back on shore.

"The Captain cannot perform divorces."

"Where did Patty go?"

Seasickness

Everyone gets seasick from time to time, generally after using a head (see page 4) that has been blocked, or eating peanut butter and bologna sandwiches that some nine-year-old made. Avoidance is the best prevention and you prevent seasickness by gulping lots of fresh air and by imbibing steady doses of alcohol. This is the real reason sailing people drink so much. Old salts only get sick when they stop drinking.

Seasickness

Four Rules of Prevention

1. Gulp lots of fresh air

2. Stay out of blocked heads

3. Drink moderately but constantly

4. Always vomit to leeward. This won't help you, but it will prevent others from getting sick.

"I know we're trying to save water, but I'd appreciate it if next time you'd wash your hair in the domestic beer."

Stan always knows when he's had enough to drink.

"You're right, the boat has stopped rocking."

"These inland waterways create a whole new
set of hazards."

Learning to Sail

Learning to sail is essentially simple and can be easily learned in an afternoon or two. What takes a lifetime is learning sailing terminology so you can call everything by some name only other sailors who have put in a lifetime of study will understand. Aback, Abaft, Abeam, Halyard, Hanks, and Hard-a 'Lee, who knows what they are talking about.

"Very funny, very funny."

"You can cast off now."

"Will you stop mumbling, I can't understand
a word you're saying.

Basic Sailing Terminology

Heel	Back part of shoe which keeps you from sliding off when boat tilts.
Poop	What a little kid leaves in the head because he or she can't figure out how to flush.
Port	As in "There's no port <u>left</u> in the bottle."
Starboard	What you see <u>right</u> away when there's no port left.
Bow	The part that bangs into other boats and rocks.
Stern	The part you run to when the bow hits something.
*Leeward	Downwind
*Windward	Toward the wind.

But these two change when you turn to port or starboard which has something to do with Hard a 'Lee and jibing so you'd better fathom all this or you'll be thwarted amidships.

"Ladies, you're on the wrong side again."

"Did you see the size of that thing?"

"You fellows have any ice?"

How to Appear Nautical in Bars

Sailing is a very social activity and much of it takes place in bars when ashore. You'd better look nautical if you want to be accepted.

The four keys to looking nautical are:

1. Dress nautical – blue blazer, caps, Irish sweaters & boat shoes are good.

2. Talk nautical – see page 18.

3. Smell nautical or at least salty which is pretty easy if you've ever used most on-board showers.

4. Drink too much.

"No problem, Phyllis loves to clean fish."

"Honey, have you seen my bait?"

"Give it a little gas, honey.
I think we've got it loose."

Sex and Sailing

Sex has always been closely associated with sailing because sailing costs lots of money and everyone knows money is the one true aphrodisiac. If you don't believe me, just take a look at all the "beautiful people" who adorn most boats. The whole earth would be populated by these people if actual intercourse wasn't so difficult on boats.

Sex and Sailing

Sex is difficult on a boat because:

---

1. Cabins are tiny permitting only one, or at most, two positions without banging your head on something hard and sharp.

---

2. Crew and guests can hear everything.

---

3. A significant percentage of sailors are too drunk, hung over or too seasick to do it at any particular moment.

Anchoring and Mooring

No one really knows what's on the bottom of the sea any more than anyone knows why metal boats float. Rather than risk anchoring on, say, a rusty old supermarket cart, or some other rubbish and having your expensive boat float away, always try to tie up to a mooring.

Picking up a mooring is best done when no one is looking.

"Certainly you have a reciprocal agreement
with our club."

"Oh, don't worry. The mosquitoes at this mooring
can't fit thru the portholes."

Cruising

When you think of cruising, you think of relaxing and carefree and worryless times. What you get, of course, is the constant specter of a watery grave and a captain yelling at you to conserve water. Water, fresh water so plentiful at home, but on shipboard limited to 30 or 100 gallons for drinking, washing and cooking, so you're afraid to brush your teeth or take a real shower knowing everyone else on board is listening to every drop you use. Who can relax when this most basic element of life is so rationed?

Running out of beer also causes lots of anxiety.

"Patrick promises never to flush another fishie
down the toilet."

"But we don't know anyone in this harbor."

"These European tourists are so uninhibited."

Welcome Aboard

When you're a guest on someone else's boat, it's nice to bring a little gift. To help in the selection, I've listed a few proper and questionable ones.

Sailing Gifts That are Proper:

1. Beer
2. Chocolate
3. Foul weather gear including plastic garbage bags
4. Anything salty – salty language, salty stories, salty pretzels

Sailing Gifts that are Questionable

1. Pets

2. Survival gear

3. Airline vomit bags

4. Books like this, unless autographed
   (for autograph send $5.00 cash to H. Kavet, Ivory Tower
   Publishing, 125 Walnut Street, Watertown, MA 02172.
   It'll be worth a fortune someday.)

"Wind picked up last night."

"Men, the good news is there's a double ration of rum for all hands. The bad news is the captain wants to go water skiing."

"Give him the sandwich, Larry.
Give him the sandwich."

"Watch out everybody. Here comes another one."

Capsizing

Capsizing is an ever present danger in all unballasted boats. Boats capsize because of strong winds or dumb crew errors. Captains are Captains because they never make these dumb errors. It is unusual for boats to capsize in anything but freezing cold water. If the Captain catches a cold from the freezing water he or she blames it on some hapless crew member. When you read about single-handed ocean voyages, it is mainly because of these Captain-Crew conflicts.

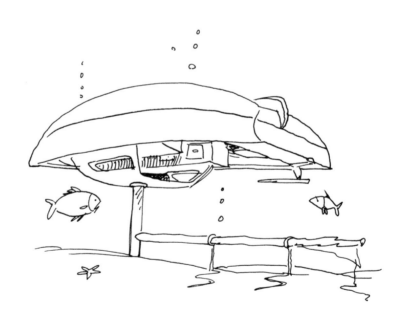

"Has anyone seen Sinbad?"

"Winston was right. It sleeps twelve."

"Very funny, very funny."

"It's sure great to have Babu guarding the boat."

"Please keep it steady, darling. I'm doing my nails."

Monsters in the Ice Chest

There are often monsters that live in a boat's ice chest. These monsters give off terrible odors and exude some sort of goo that coats the bottom of the compartment. Most sailors feel ice chest monsters live by devouring beer cans as there is no other explanation for the disappearance of these cans.

"Don't be silly, dear. There's no monster
in the ice chest."

"His idea of nautical adventure is sharing
a bathtub with you."

"Sorry I'm late. Been waiting long?"

"Can't tell. The section we need is right under
the coffee stain."

"Always watch out for the boom."

Using the Head at Night

We've explained the pumping and valves and handles that make a seagoing toilet work. Well, kiddies, you should know that all these pieces of machinery make a God-awful noise and if you use the head during the night you will awaken everyone on board. It's your choice, hold it till morning, wake the whole boat, or neglect to flush and blame it on someone else the next day.

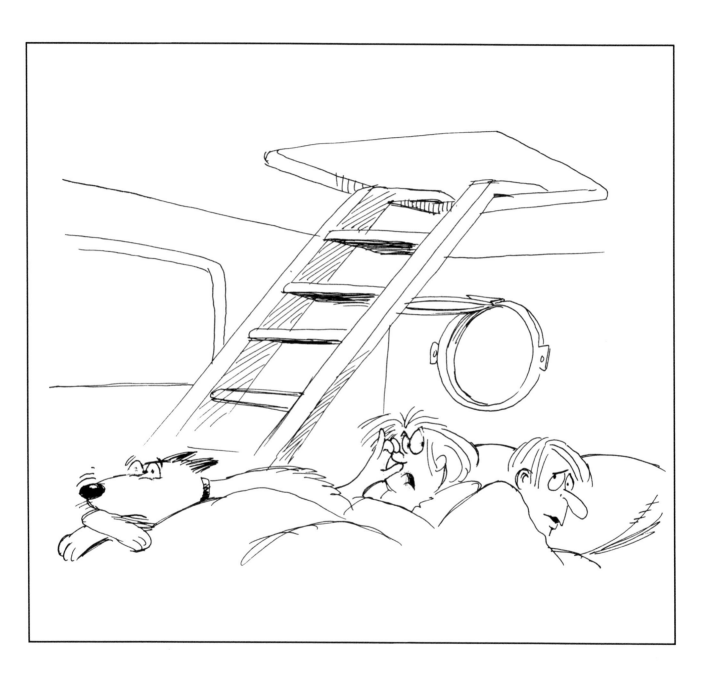

"The dog did not do it."

"It's not that kind of a bar."

"For God's sake, Winthrop, we all know winches
are expensive."

"Honey, no one's going to notice you missed the mooring 7 times."

"I've told you a hundred times, it's a HEAD, not a toilet, and a GALLEY, not a kitchen. Now get it straight or I'll shove you through one of those little round windows.

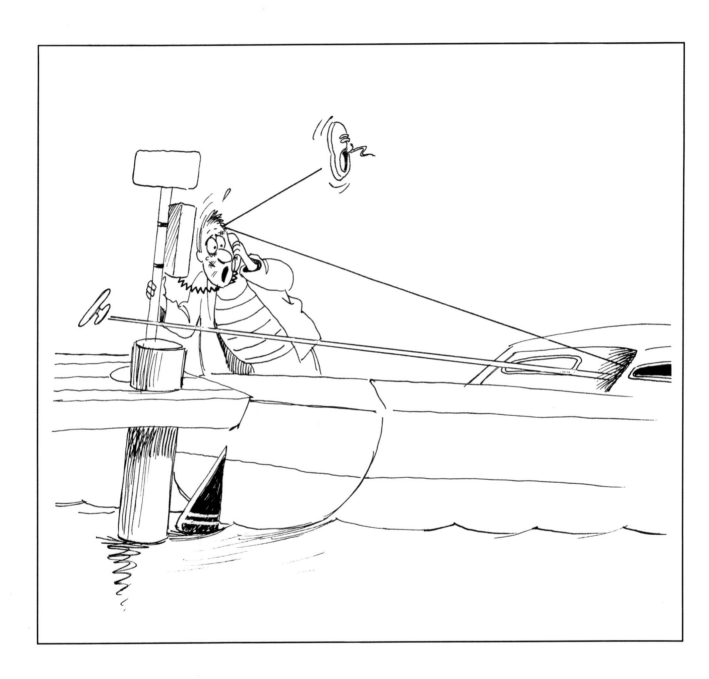

"Hello, PMS Hotline?"

"You won't get away with this, Ron."

The Tangle Gremlins get loose in the line locker.

"Cocktail hour is not a destination."

These other books are available at many fine stores.

#2350 Sailing. Using the head at night • Sex & Sailing • Monsters in the Ice Chest • How to look nautical in bars and much more nautical nonsense.

#2351 Computers. Where computers really are made • How to understand computer manuals without reading them • Sell your old $2,000,000 computer for $60 • Why computers are always lonely and much more solid state computer humor.

#2352 Cats. Living with cat hair • The advantages of kitty litter • Cats that fart • How to tell if you've got a fat cat.

#2353 Tennis. Where do lost balls go? • Winning the psychological game • Catching your breath • Perfecting wood shots.

#2354 Bowling. A book of bowling cartoons that covers: Score sheet cheaters • Boozers • Women who show off • Facing your team after a bad box and much more.

#2355 Parenting. Understanding the Tooth Fairy • 1000 ways to toilet train • Informers and tattle tales • Differences between little girls and little boys • And enough other information and laughs to make every parent wet their beds.

#2356 Fitness. T-shirts that will stop them from laughing at you • Earn big money with muscles • Sex and Fitness • Lose weight with laughter from this book.

#2357 Golf. Playing the psychological game • Going to the toilet in the rough • How to tell a real golfer • Some of the best golf cartoons ever printed.

#2358 Fishing. Handling 9" mosquitoes • Raising worms in your microwave oven • Neighborhood targets for fly casting practice • How to get on a first name basis with the Coast Guard plus even more.

#2359 Bathrooms. Why people love their bathroom • Great games to help pass the time on toilets • A frank discussion of bathroom odors • Plus lots of other stuff everyone out of diapers should know.

#2360 Biking. Why the wind is always against you • Why bike clothes are so tight • And lots of other stuff about what goes thunk, thunk, thunk when you pedal.

#2361 Running. How to "go" in the woods • Why running shoes cost more than sneakers • Keeping your lungs from bursting by letting the other guy talk.

Ivory Tower Publishing Co., Inc.   125 Walnut St., PO Box 9132, Watertown, MA 02272-9132
Telephone #: (617) 923-1111   Fax #: (617) 923-8839